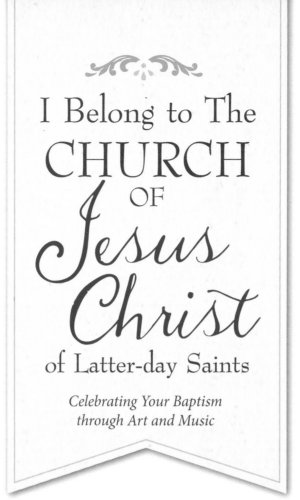

I Belong to The
CHURCH
OF
Jesus
Christ
of Latter-day Saints

Celebrating Your Baptism
through Art and Music

Text by Janice Kapp Perry

Front Cover: *Baptism* © Simon Dewey, courtesy Altus Fine Art. For print information, visit www.altusfineart.com or call 801-763-9788.

Music:

1.	*The Church of Jesus Christ*	CS, 77 Words and music: Janice Kapp Perry © 1989 IRI
2.	*Baptism*	CS, 100 Words: Mabel Jones Gabbott; Music: Crawford Gates © 1969 IRI
3.	*When I Am Baptized*	CS, 103 Words and music: Nita Dale Milner © 1989 IRI
4.	*I'm Trying to Be Like Jesus*	CS, 78 Words and music: Janice Kapp Perry © 1980 Janice Kapp Perry
5.	*Come, Follow Me*	Hymns, no. 116 Words: John Nicholson; Music: Samuel McBurney
6.	*The Holy Ghost*	CS, 105 Words and music: Jeanne P. Lawler © 1977 IRI
7.	*Let the Holy Spirit Guide*	Hymns, no. 143 Words: Penelope Moody Allen © 1985 IRI; Music: Martin Shaw © 1915 J. Curwen & Sons
8.	*Keep the Commandments*	CS, 146–7 Words and music: Barbara A. McConochie © 1975 IRI
9.	*The Church of Jesus Christ* (minus track)	CS, 77 Music: Janice Kapp Perry © 1989 IRI

Cover and interior designed by Christina Marcano
Cover design © 2017 Covenant Communications, Inc.
Published by Covenant Communications, Inc.
American Fork, Utah

Printed in China
First Printing: October 2017

24 23 22 20 19 18 17   10 9 8 7 6 5 4 3 2 1

Baptism (Girl) ISBN: 978-1-52440-362-1
Baptism (Boy) ISBN: 978-1-52440-361-4

I Belong to The

CHURCH

OF

Jesus

Christ

of Latter-day Saints

Simon Dewey

I
know
WHO I AM.

I know

GOD'S

plan.

I'll
follow
HIM
in faith.

I believe
in the
Savior,

JESUS CHRIST.

I'll honor
HIS NAME.

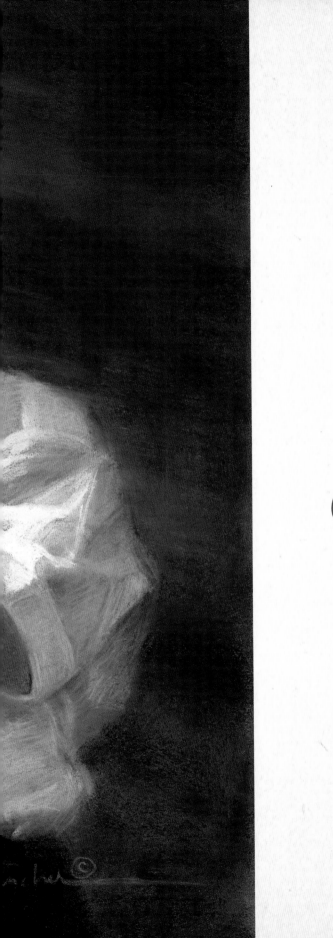

This is the
CHURCH
OF
*Jesus
Christ*

And it
STANDS
FOR
Good
and
TRUTH
and
right.

I

WILL FOLLOW

His

teachings,

honor
His
DEAR
NAME.

I will

LOVE
HIM,
serve Him,

His
truth
PROCLAIM.

I'll do
WHAT
is
right.

I'll

follow

His light.

His

truth

I WILL

PROCLAIM.

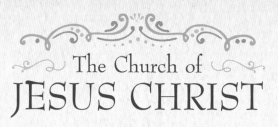

The Church of
JESUS CHRIST

(Two-Part)

Words and Music by
Janice Kapp Perry

With conviction (♩ = 116)

Sing #1 alone, #2 alone, then #1 and #2 together

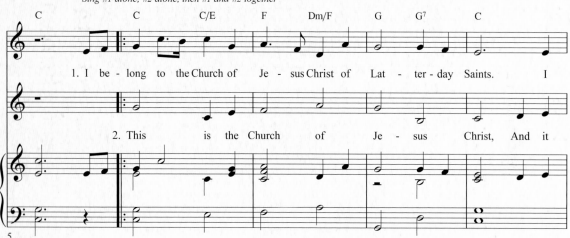

1. I be - long to the Church of Je - sus Christ of Lat - ter-day Saints. I

2. This is the Church of Je - sus Christ, And it

know who I am. I know God's plan. I'll fol - low Him in faith. I be - lieve in the Sav - ior,

stands for good and truth and right. I will fol - low His

Je - sus Christ. I'll hon - or His name. I'll do what is right; I'll

teach - ings, hon - or His dear name. I will love Him,

15

Repeat twice

(3rd time)

fol - low His light. His truth I will pro - claim. I be - I'll do what is right, I'll

serve Him, His truth pro - claim. I'll do what is right, I'll

(3rd time)

19

cresc.

fol - low His light, His truth I will pro - claim.

cresc.

fol - low His light, His truth I will pro - claim.

cresc.

24

Simon De

BAPTISM

"The Church of Jesus Christ" is a beautiful song that helps us express joy over the decision to be baptized.

Baptism is one of the most important things you can do: it is required for you to enter the kingdom of heaven and return to live with your Heavenly Father. Jesus told us, "Except a man be born of water and of the Spirit, he cannot enter into the kingdom of God" (John 3:5).

When you are baptized—born of water—your wrongs are washed away and you are completely clean. What a wonderful feeling! And you are following Christ's example. Jesus was perfect; He never committed a sin. But He went to His cousin John the Baptist and asked to be baptized so He could show *us* the way. He wanted us to know what we need to do. Baptism is required to get into heaven, and that is true for everyone, even Jesus.

Following your baptism, you are confirmed—"born of the Spirit." At that time, you receive the Holy Ghost to be your companion and your helper throughout your life.

Several important things happen when you are baptized. You become a member of The Church of Jesus Christ of Latter-day Saints, and you take Jesus's name upon you. That means you follow Him and believe in His teachings and do your very best to obey Him. It is one of the most meaningful things you will ever do in this life. When you are baptized, you are telling Heavenly Father you want to keep His commandments, repent when you make a mistake, and come back to live with Him when your life on this earth is finished.

You also make important covenants, or two-way promises. You promise that you will bear others' burdens, mourn with those who mourn, and comfort those who stand in need of comfort. That means you will look for ways to help others who feel sad or discouraged, and you will try your best to be a good friend. You also promise to stand as a witness of God at all times and in all places; that means you will always let others know that you believe in Him.

> After you are baptized, Jesus will be your guide and your helper. He will comfort you and show you the way. You could not ask for a better friend in all the world!

His part of the promise is wonderful! He promises that if you do those things, you will always have His Spirit to be with you. He will be your guide and your helper; He will comfort you and show you the way. You could not ask for a better friend in all the world!

Every week when you take the sacrament, you will be reminded of the covenants you made at baptism. You will promise again to do all those things you promised when you were baptized. You can be sure that your Savior will never forget you—and by being baptized and keeping those covenants, you are telling Him how much you love Him and are promising you will never forget Him.

ART CREDITS

Baptism (Girl) © Simon Dewey, courtesy Altus Fine Art. For print information, visit www.altusfineart.com or call 801-763-9788.

I'm Trying to Be Like Jesus © Greg K. Olsen. By arrangement with Greg Olsen Art, Inc. For more information about art prints by Greg Olsen, please visit www.GregOlsen.com or call 1-800-352-0107.

Along the Cliffs © Robert Duncan. For more information, visit www.robertduncanstudios.com or call 1-800-282-0954.

Hand in Hand © Greg K. Olsen. By arrangement with Greg Olsen Art, Inc. For more information about art prints by Greg Olsen, please visit www.GregOlsen.com or call 1-800-352-0107.

Come and See © Del Parson; for print information, visit www.delparson.com.

Here's the Church © Kathy Fincher. For more information, visit www.kathyfincher.com.

I Love to See the Temple © Simon Dewey, courtesy Altus Fine Art. For print information, visit www.altusfineart.com or call 801-763-9788.

I Can Choose the Right—Scriptures © Simon Dewey, courtesy Altus Fine Art. For print information, visit www.altusfineart.com or call 801-763-9788.

Jesus Loves Me © Kathy Fincher. For more information, visit www.kathyfincher.com.

Seeking the Spirit © Greg K. Olsen. By arrangement with Greg Olsen Art, Inc. For more information about art prints by Greg Olsen, please visit www.GregOlsen.com or call 1-800-352-0107.

Don't Forget to Pray © Greg K. Olsen. By arrangement with Greg Olsen Art, Inc. For more information about art prints by Greg Olsen, please visit www.GregOlsen.com or call 1-800-352-0107.

The Light of the World © Simon Dewey, courtesy Altus Fine Art. For print information, visit www.altusfineart.com or call 801-763-9788.

The Millionth Missionary © Rebecca Lee Peery.

Baptism (Boy) © Simon Dewey, courtesy Altus Fine Art. For print information, visit www.altusfineart.com or call 801-763-9788.